THE KALEIDOSCOPE KID

THE KALEIDOSCOPE KID

Focusing on the Strengths of Children with Asperger Syndrome and High-Functioning Autism

by Elaine Marie Larson

Illustrated by Vivian Strand

APC

P.O. Box 23173
Shawnee Mission, Kansas 66283-0173
www.asperger.net

© 2007 Autism Asperger Publishing Co.
P.O. Box 23173
Shawnee Mission, Kansas 66283-0173
www.asperger.net

Publisher's Cataloging-in-Publication

Larson, Elaine M.
    The kaleidoscope kid : focusing on the strengths of children with Asperger syndrome and high functioning autism / by Elaine Marie Larson. -- 1st ed. -- Shawnee Mission, Kan : Autism Asperger Pub. Co., 2007.

        p. ; cm.

        ISBN-13: 978-1-931282-41-3
        ISBN-10: 1-931282-41-2
        LCCN: 2007921490

        1. Asperger's syndrome in children--Juvenile literature. 2. Autism in children--Juvenile literature. 3. Autistic children--Juvenile literature. I. Title.

RJ506.A9 L37 2007
618.92/858832--dc22   0703

This book is designed in Myriad and Bonkers.

Printed in the United States of America.

DEDICATION

To my grandchildren Sam, Jenna, Ellie and Mia. Each of you is like the view through a kaleidoscope – ever changing but infinitely unique and wonderful.

The Kaleidoscope Kid is written to remind children with Asperger Syndrome or high-functioning autism of their many special gifts and to make others aware of them, too.

These children possess a kaleidoscope of intellectual strengths and unique personality traits. Their outlook and creative ways are as variable and colorful as the view through a kaleidoscope.

Table of Contents

I Am Truthful

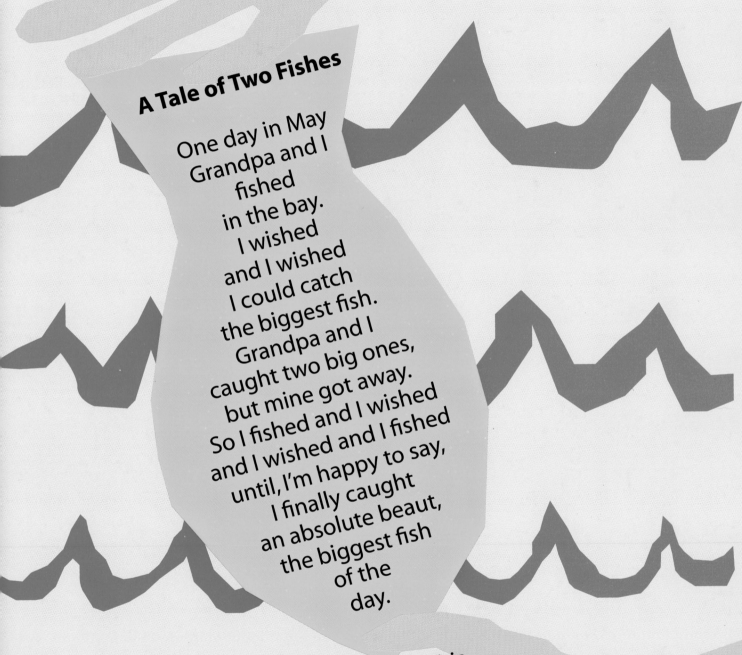

A Tale of Two Fishes

One day in May
Grandpa and I
fished
in the bay.
I wished
and I wished
I could catch
the biggest fish.
Grandpa and I
caught two big ones,
but mine got away.
So I fished and I wished
and I wished and I fished
until, I'm happy to say,
I finally caught
an absolute beaut,
the biggest fish
of the
day.

It was as big as this ...

HONEST!

AND IT DIDN'T GET AWAY!

1

I Am Helpful

A Holiday Nightmare

I dreamed I aided Cupid
but my arrow went astray.
I freed Thanksgiving turkeys,
who moved in with me to stay.

Mother's Day I baked a pie
but at measuring I'm a chump.
Father's Day I washed Dad's car
though his windows were not up.

I woke from slumber shaking,
thankful nightmares are quite rare,
but then I saw ten turkeys
Eating stuffing from my chair.

E

I Enjoy Word Play

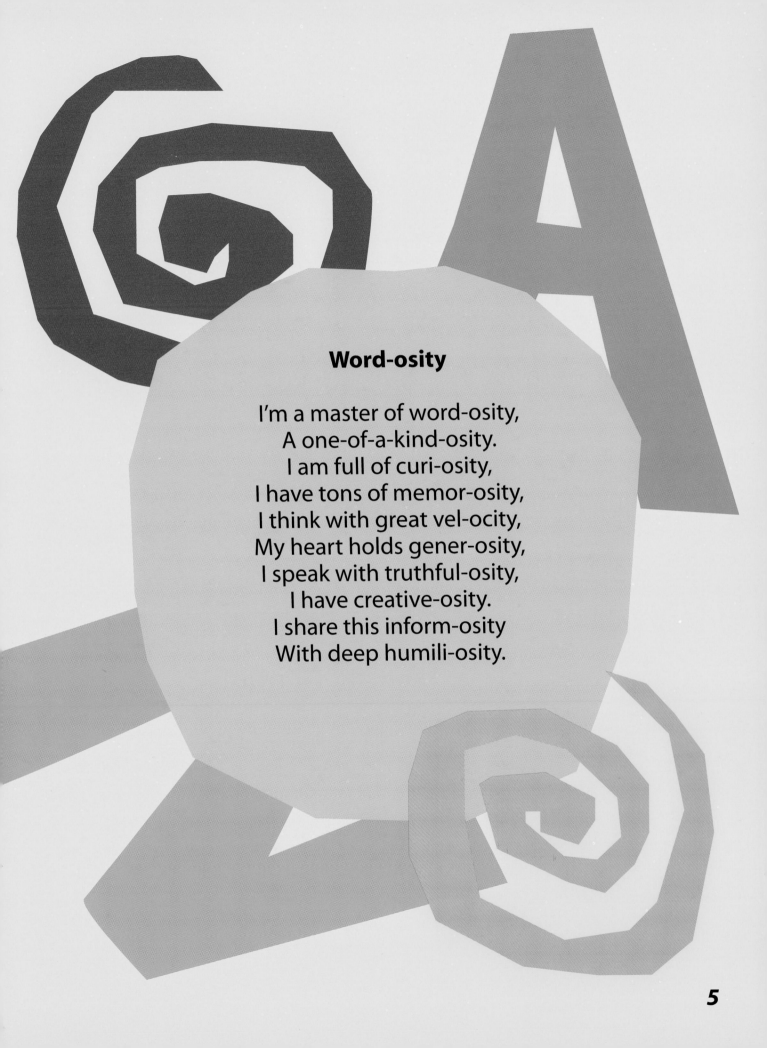

Word-osity

I'm a master of word-osity,
A one-of-a-kind-osity.
I am full of curi-osity,
I have tons of memor-osity,
I think with great vel-ocity,
My heart holds gener-osity,
I speak with truthful-osity,
I have creative-osity.
I share this inform-osity
With deep humili-osity.

K

I Am Knowledgeable

Dinosaurus Infomaurus

Stegosaurus, Supersaurus,
Seismosaurus, too.
The herbivores are hungry
for their vegetarian stew.

Giganotosaurus, Spinosaurus,
Tyrannosaurus-Rex.
The carnivores are hungry.
Is a tender T-bone next?

A

I Love Animals

My Menagerie

I love my dog,
My cat and snake,
I love my goldfish, too.
My squirrel,
Rat and beaver
Play hide-and-seek
And chew.

The ferret
and the parrot
Are my friends
Each day anew,
and the elephant
Is charming though she
Grew and grew and grew.

I love to feed
and groom them,
Even pick up
Pooh … oh, phew!
But there's no room
in my bed for me
When our play is through.

I Am a Loyal Friend

An *Almost* True Blue Friend

When you dare go
in the jungle,
I'll be there.

Should you ignore
the sign "BEWARE,"
I'll be there.

If you find
the lion's lair,
I'll be there.

When his roar
gives you a scare,
I'll be there.

But
if the lion
chases you,
I'm outa there!

E

I Am Enthusiastic

Summer Rules!

Holy mackerel,
Holy cow!
The sun's come up,
It's morning now!

Wowie, zowie,
Yippee skippy!
Yay, hurray,
Yee-haw, okay!
Uh-huh, wheeeee,
Yesss! Whoopee!
Awesome, wow,
Bravo, yow!

Awright, it's cool,
Summer rules!
Excellent,
Let's hit the pool!

Splash!!!

Mmhmm!!!!

I Am Imaginative

Right at the top.
Is revealed
Whodunit
Unfortunately,
I stopped.
And at the top
Up the page
I wrote a mystery

**"Up!
Bottoms"**

(Read poem from the bottom up)

15

I Am Detail-Oriented

Crossing My T's

I make tall letters tall
And small letters small.
I remember to cross my t's.
And the words must alight
on the page left to right.
Perfection
Is key to me!

(Get out a mirror to read this.)

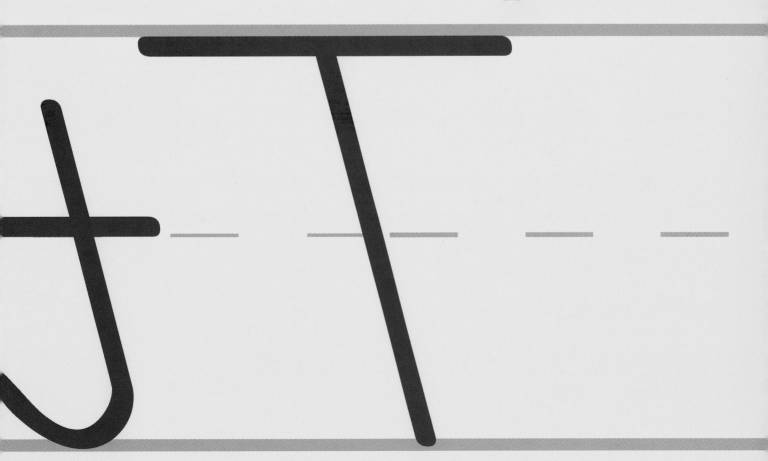

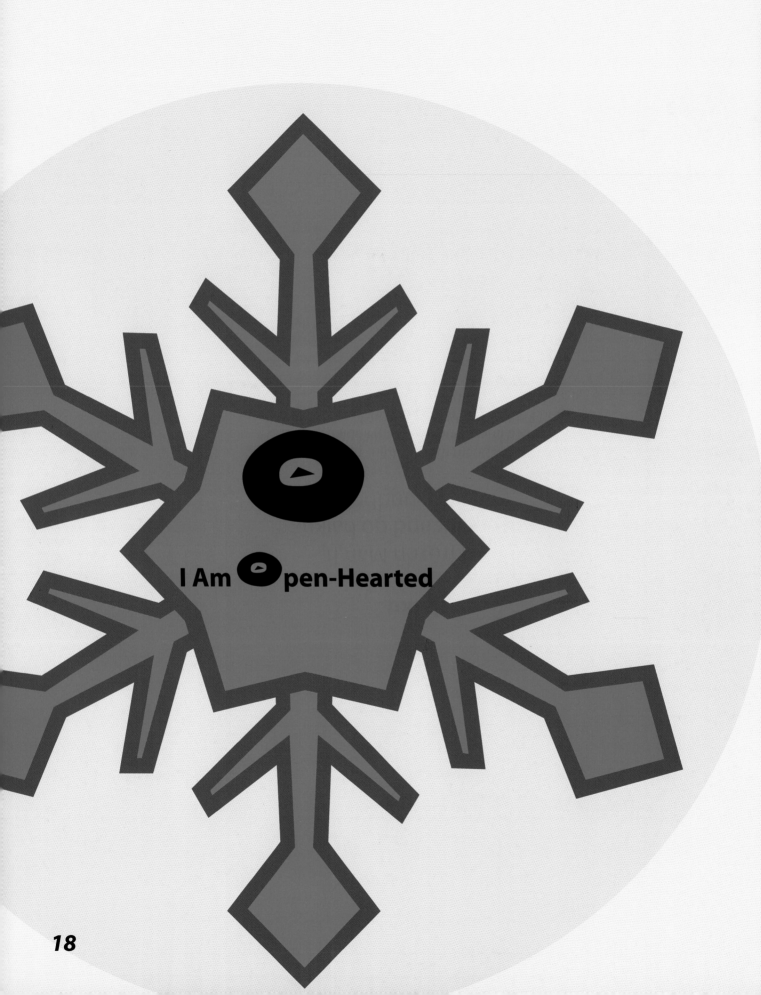

I Am Open-Hearted

Haiku

Flu in frozen March,
You shiver and go haiku.
I say, "Gesundheit."

(A haiku is a poem that contains three generally unrhymed lines. It includes 17 syllables, in lines of 5, 7, and 5 syllables. Haikus often include a subject that links nature to human nature.)

S

I Am a Special Person

Changing Places

If bananas and cherries
Could trade shapes and sizes,
Exchange skins and colors
Creating disguises …

Would you peel the cherries
to eat them for brunch,
or munch red peels
off bananas for lunch?

Bananas and cherries
Don't need to charade.
They nourish and delight
Just the way they were made.

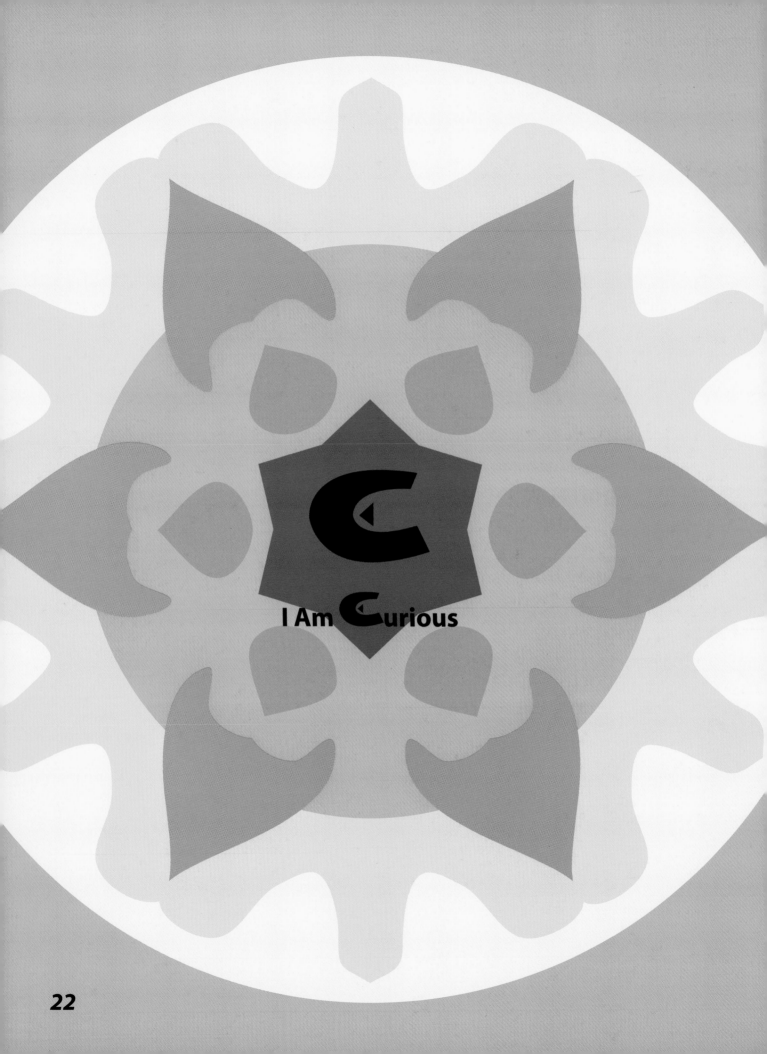

I Am Curious

The Box on the Floor

That box
on the floor …
What's it for?
Seen it before?
Is it for me?
What can it be?
Who is it from?
When did it come?
Hey, may I open it,
okay?

Clip. Snip, rip …
AAACK!!!

Do you have a clue
what it will do?
Why's it so hairy
and terribly scary?
Isn't it clear
I don't want
this thing here?
Isn't it strange?
May I arrange
to send it away?

What do you say?
Can I mail it
in that box
on the floor?
Is that what it's for?

I Am a One-of-a-Kind

A Rhythm All My Own

Row after row
the marchers go.
Right, left, right,
Formation tight.

I twirl around.
Swirl and bound,
My own direction.
Sheer perfection.

P

I Am Persistent

(The following poem refers to the yoga "tree" pose.)

Tree Pose

I
stand
tall
breathing
slowly,
deeply,
focusing
on being still.

I
plant
my roots
firmly in the earth.

I
reach
for the sky,
breathing
slowly,
deeply.
Swaying,
waving,
teetering.
T-I-M-B-E-R!

I
stand
tall.
Breathing
slowly,
deeply …

E

I Am Excellent

I Am Me

If I were a piano,
I'd be a
concert grand.
If I were a beach,
I'd be
Hawaiian sand.

If I were a palace,
I'd be London's
Buckingham.
If I were a wall,
I'd be
the Hoover Dam.

But I am me.
I'll always be
the best at
What I'm best at,
Which is being
Excellent Me!

K

I Have a Keen Mind

Just Ask Me

Did you know
There are lizards that fly,
And snakes, fish and frogs
That soar through the sky?
It's an amazing thing
How some creatures
Can fly without wings.
How can it be?
Just ask me.

I Am an Information Detective

Upside-Down Critters

During the day
when predators prey,
bats hang still,
hidden away.

There are
upside-down
jellyfish, more similar
to plants than fish.

Dwarf catfish
will sleep all day,
but nocturnally,
they eat and play.

Wound round branches
of forest trees,
sloths munch leaves
unabashedly.

One last critter's
upside-down.
It's only me
hanging 'round.

I Am Dependable

34

Scores of Chores

Walk the dog
Feed the fishes

Clear the table
Do the dishes

Brush my teeth
Tidy drawers

Take out trash –
An icky chore

Hang up clothes
Water plants

Run to store
Write my aunts

Dependable,
A fitting label

Last four letters
Spell out **able**!

Also by Elaine Larson and Vivian Strand

From A to Z – Discover the Unique Characteristics and Abilities of Children with Asperger Syndrome and High-Functioning Autism

I Am Utterly Unique

Celebrating the Strengths of Children
with Asperger Syndrome
and High-Functioning Autism

by Elaine Marie Larson;
illustrated by Vivian Strand

Discover the unique characteristics and abilities of children with Asperger Syndrome and high-functioning autism – from A to Z. This book, laid out in an A-to-Z format, celebrates the extraordinary gifts and unique perspectives that children with ASD possess. Each page of this playful alphabet book presents one of these children's many talents and abilities. The kid-friendly illustrations and clever text create a positive portrayal of children with ASD. Designed to help children with ASD grow in self-awareness of their many capabilities, *I Am Utterly Unique* also encourages dialogue with siblings, friends, parents and teachers.

Code 9961 (Hardcover)   **Price $18.95**

Other children's books published by the Autism Asperger Publishing Company

All About My Brother

Sarah Peralta
Code 9914
(Hardcover)
Price: $16.95

When My Worries Get Too Big! A Relaxation Book for Children Who Live with Anxiety

Kari Dunn Buron
Code 9962
Price $16.95

Sundays with Matthew: A Young Boy with Autism and an Artist Share Their Sketchbooks

Jeanette Lesada and Matthew Lancelle
Code 9954 (Hardcover)
Price: $17.95

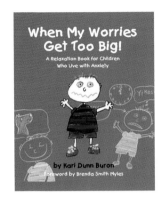

My Best Friend Will

Jamie Lowell and Tara Tuchel
Code 9947
(Hardcover)
Price: $21.95

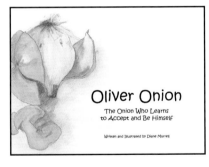

Oliver Onion: The Onion Who Learns to Accept and Be Himself

Diane Murrell
Code 9939
(Hardcover)
Price: $16.95

This Is Asperger Syndrome

Elisa Gagnon and Brenda Smith Myles; illustrated by Sachi Tahara

Code 9903
Price: $12.95

Amazingly ... Alphie: Understanding and Accepting Different Ways of Being

Roz Espin; illustrated by Beverley Ransom
Code 9927
Price: $15.95

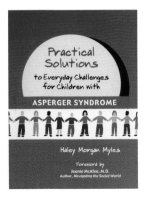

Practical Solutions to Everyday Challenges for Children with Asperger Syndrome

Haley Morgan Myles
Code 9917
Price: $12.95

Place your order online at www.asperger.net, or call toll-free: 877-AS Publish (877-277-8254)

AAPC

Autism Asperger Publishing Co.
P.O. Box 23173
Shawnee Mission, Kansas 66283-0173
www.asperger.net